Twenty-Third Publications
A Division of Bayard
185 Willow Street
P.O. Box 180
Mystic, CT 06355
(860) 536-2611 or (800) 321-0411
www.twentythirdpublications.com
ISBN: 1-58595-382-2

Published in Canada by
Novalis
Business Office:
49 Front Street East, 2nd Floor
Toronto, Ontario, Canada
M5E 1B3
Phone: 1-877-702-7773 or (416) 363-3303
Fax: 1-877-702-7775 or (416) 363-9409
Email: novalis-inc.ca
www.novalis.ca
ISBN: 2-89507-627-8

Quotations were chosen by Rev. Vincent Cabanac, A.A.,
editor in chief of *La Documentation Catholique*,
published by Bayard in Paris, France.
Prayers and Actions were written by Gwen Costello,
author of *Blessed Are You! A Prayerbook for Catholics*
(Twenty-Third Publications).
Photos were provided by *Pope John Paul II Cultural Center*
in Washington, D.C.

WALKING
IN THE *Light*

30 Days with Pope John Paul II

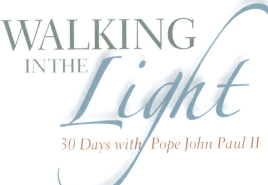

Contents

Introduction

This small book contains many priceless gems of spiritual wisdom from one of the greatest spiritual leaders of our time, Pope John Paul II. From Day One to Day Thirty, the Pope challenges, invites, coaxes, and encourages us to give ourselves to Jesus Christ completely. Nothing else will make us happy, nothing else will last.

Each of the Pope's daily reflections center on one of the virtues and is meant to be prayerfully pondered, read and re-read, until it takes root in our hearts. The reflections are warm, tender, and heartfelt, so much so that love for Christ comes through on every page.

Each daily reflection is accompanied by a Scripture passage (for further reflection), a prayer, and an action response to the Pope's daily challenge to live a virtuous life.

May these thirty days with Pope John Paul II inspire you to embrace the Christian life more fully so that the light of Christ can shine brightly through you to all the world.

"Because Jesus is
the Light, we too
become light
when we proclaim
him. This is the
heart of the
Christian mission
to which each of
us has been
called through
Baptism and
Confirmation.
We are called to
make the light of
Christ shine
brightly in the
world."

✠ ST. LOUIS, 1999

» Scripture

I am the light of the world. Whoever follows me will never walk in darkness.

■ JOHN: 8:12

» Pray

Loving Savior, my light is not so bright when it comes to proclaiming your presence. My heart is not so big when it comes to sharing with others. Light my way and enlarge my heart that I might share your light with others in all my thoughts, words, and deeds.

» Act

I will try to be conscious of the needs of others today and offer the light of Christ by helping someone I might otherwise ignore.

3

"It is Jesus in fact that you seek when you dream of happiness. He is waiting for you when nothing else you find satisfies you. He is the beauty to which you are so attracted. ...It is Jesus who stirs in you the desire to do something great with your life."

✝ ROME, 2000

4

» Scripture

Strive first for the kingdom of heaven and all that you need will be given to you.

■ MATTHEW 6:33

» Pray

Loving Savior, I do want to find true happiness. I do want to strive first for the kingdom of heaven. Strengthen me to trust that your grace is truly all that I need. Give me your gift of happiness.

» Act

Today I will make a list of all the things that bring happiness into my life and I will try to actively bring happiness to others.

"Peace will not come as the result of our own efforts; it is not something that the world can give. It is a gift from the Lord, and to receive it we have to prepare our hearts. When conflicts arise, peace can only come through a process of reconciliation, and this requires both humility and generosity."

✝ ROME, 2001

» Scripture

Peace be with you. As God has sent me,
so I send you.

■ JOHN 20:21

» Pray

Loving Savior, you send me out to restore
peace: in my family, with my friends,
and with my coworkers. But without
your guidance I don't know how to be
a peacemaker. I'm not very courageous
when it comes to reconciling with
others. Please give me your gift of peace.

» Act

Today I want to take the first step in
reconciling with someone I have
offended. I want to offer peace instead
of anger and resentment.

Courage

"Believing in and loving God means a consistent life, lived wholly in the light of the Gospel. It means being committed to doing always what Jesus tells us…. This is not easy, it often calls for great courage in going against the trends of fashion and the opinions of the world."

✝ ROME, 1998

8

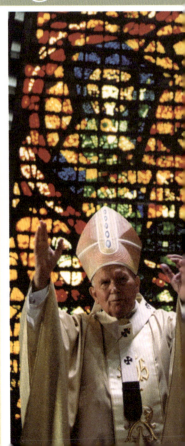

» Scripture

Stand firm, sisters and brothers, and hold
fast to the traditions that you were taught.

■ 2 THESSALONIANS 2:15

» Pray

Loving Savior, how daunting it is to do
everything in the light of the Gospel!
And yet, that's what it means to be
your follower. I want to deepen my
commitment to you and I want to open
my ears and my heart to hear what you
are asking me to do. Give me your gift
of courage.

» Act

I will try to have the courage today to
proclaim that I am a follower of Christ
through all my words and deeds.

9

"My faith, like the faith of each one of you, is not just my doing, my attachment to the truth of Christ and the Church. It is essentially and primarily the work of the Holy Spirit, a gift of his grace. The Lord gives us his Spirit to help us say 'I believe,' and then he sends us out to bear witness to him."

✝ ROME, 2000

10

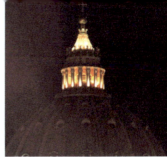

» Scripture

I always give thanks to God for all of
you, remembering your works of faith.

■ 1 THESSALONIANS 1:2–3

» Pray

Loving Savior, I do believe, but I let
everything distract me from the one
thing that matters: your presence
within me. Deepen my faith that I
might bear witness to you and your
gospel message. Give me the gift
of faith.

» Act

Throughout this day, I will acknowledge
the indwelling Christ by simply saying,
"I believe."

DAY 6 | Hope

"Although I have lived through much darkness, …I have seen enough evidence to be unshakably convinced that no difficulty, no fear is so great that it can completely suffocate the hope that springs eternal in our hearts. Do not let that hope die! Stake your life on it!"

✠ TORONTO, 2002

» Scripture

Rejoice in hope, be patient in suffering, persevere in prayer.

■ ROMANS 12:12

» Pray

Loving Savior, I trust you with all my heart and I hope to please you in all that I do. I hope, too, for eternal life. Through whatever difficulties I might have to face, help me to remember to hold on to you. Give me the gift of hope.

» Act

I will reflect today about what I hope for most deeply, and I will consider God's place in my life.

"The ability to love as God loves is offered to every Christian as a fruit of the paschal mystery of Christ's Death and Resurrection. Indeed, God the Father loves us as he loves Christ, seeing his image in us.... This image is painted within us over and over by the Holy Spirit."

✝ ROME, 1999

14

» Scripture

I give you a new commandment, that
you love one another as I have loved you.

- JOHN 13:34

» Pray

Loving Savior, I invite your Holy Spirit
to paint your image within me so
clearly that I will never forget it is there.
Help me to love others as you love me
and help me to give witness to this
great gift in all that I do. Give me the
gift of your love.

» Act

I will look for an opportunity today to
share with others how much God loves
and watches over them. I will try to
have a loving attitude in all I do.

DAY 8 | Patience

"You are going through a time of life filled with questions and uncertainties. Yet Christ is calling you and awakening in you a desire to make your life something magnificent and beautiful.... Make your commitment to Christ with patience and perseverance."

✝ DAMASCUS, 2001

» Scripture

Love is patient; love is kind; love is not envious or boastful.

■ 1 CORINTHIANS 13:4

» Pray

Loving Savior, I do have both questions and uncertainties in my life right now, and I need patience and perseverance to daily renew my commitment to you. I want to live in your presence and I want to share this gift with others. Give me your gift of patience.

» Act

I will spend time today thinking about how important patience is and how it can help me to better accept God's timeline (and not my own) for my life.

17

"Concern for those most in need springs from a decision to love the poor in a special manner. …In loving the poor, we imitate the attitude of the Lord, who during his earthly life devoted himself with special compassion to all those in spiritual and material need."

✞ ROME, 1999

» **Scripture**

As God's chosen ones, holy and
beloved, clothe yourselves with
compassion.

■ COLOSSIANS 3:12

» **Pray**

Loving Savior, help me to imitate your
compassion for those in need. May I
put myself in the place of those who
suffer from poverty, war, drought, and
hunger, that I might carry their suffering
in my heart and do something about it.
Give me your gift of compassion.

» **Act**

I will try to be conscious of the needs of
the poor today and I will take a specific
action on their behalf.

"Beloved! The Lord has given you a heart open to the widest horizons: do not be afraid to commit your life completely to the service of Christ and the Gospel! Listen to him as he says again today: 'The harvest is abundant, but the laborers are few.'"

✞ ROME, 1994

» Scripture

Like good stewards of the manifold grace of God, serve one another with whatever gifts each of you has received.

■ 1 PETER 4:10

» Pray

Loving Savior, I want to open my heart to the widest horizons, but I always seem to hold back. I am afraid that I will have to give too much. Help me learn to trust that you will never ask more of me than I can give. I need your gift of generosity.

» Act

I will try to use my God-given gifts with someone in need today, and I will pray often for the gift of a generous heart.

21

"People are made
for happiness.
Rightly then,
you thirst for
happiness. Christ
has the answer to
this desire of
yours. But he asks
you to trust him.
True joy is a
victory, something
that can't be had
without a long
and difficult
struggle. Christ
holds the secret of
this victory."

✠ TORONTO, 2002

» ### Scripture

Rejoice in the Lord always; again I say rejoice. Let your gentleness be known to everyone. Christ is near.

■ PHILIPPIANS 4:4-5

» ### Pray

Loving Savior, I do rejoice that you are with me always. It's hard to rejoice though when difficulties come my way. Help me to trust that you will lead me to victory and to eternal happiness. Give me your gift of joy.

» ### Act

Today I will try to give joy to someone who is suffering, to lighten the burden he or she is carrying with a heartfelt smile.

"Dear brothers and sisters, our Christian communities must become genuine 'schools' of prayer, where the meeting with Christ is expressed not just in imploring help but also in thanksgiving, praise, adoration, contemplation, listening and ardent devotion."

✝ ROME, 2001

» Scripture

Pray without ceasing and give thanks to
God in all circumstances.

■ 1 THESSALONIANS 5:17-18

» Pray

Loving Savior, I want to "pray always"
by being open to your Holy Spirit within me. Help me to be still, to be ready
to do all that you ask of me. I praise
you, I thank you, I love you. Give me
the gift of a prayerful heart.

» Act

Throughout my day today, I will try to
make prayer a priority, even if I only
have time for simple words like "Be
with me, God, and watch over me."

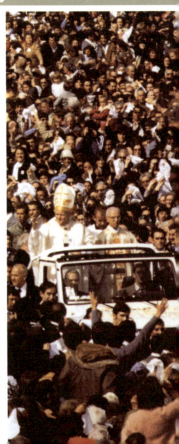

"Bear witness to Christ in today's society. Become builders of the civilization of love and truth. The construction of such a civilization requires strong and persevering individuals.... This is the first step toward a new unity, a unity that transcends the political order yet enlightens it."

✝ DENVER, 1993

26

» ### Scripture

The glory you have given me, Father,
I have given them, so that they may be
one as we are one.

■ JOHN 17:22

» ### Pray

Loving Savior, I would gladly join a
civilization of love and truth, if only I
didn't have to "construct" it myself. I
am not so strong and persevering, but I
ask for your grace to make me so. May
we all be united in you as we seek a
better world. I need the gift of unity.

» ### Act

I will do nothing today to cause division
among others, but rather I will look for
ways to bring together family members,
coworkers, and friends.

27

"Give a forceful
witness of love for
life, which is
God's gift.
...Be 'prophets of
life'! Be such by
your words and
deeds, ...and by
concretely helping
those who need
you, and who
might be tempted
to resign
themselves to
despair without
your help."

✞ ROME, 1996

» ### Scripture

You are witnesses of all that I have taught.
Go into the world and proclaim the good
news to all of creation.

■ MARK 16:15

» ### Pray

Loving Savior, I want to be a prophet
of life: to defend the unborn, to take a
stand against aggression, to safeguard
the environment, but so far I have not
been a courageous witness. Guide me
and strengthen me with your grace. I
need the gift of witness.

» ### Act

I will spend a few moments today
thinking about how I can be a better
"prophet for life" in all its forms, and
thus give witness to Christ.

29

"Your mission in today's world is to faithfully safe-guard certain important values: total religious freedom; the respect for human life at every stage; ...the importance of the family; the appreciation of cultural diversity."

✝ CZESTOCHOWA, 1991

"Be faithful witnesses to Christ, as difficult as this might be."

✝ ROME, 2000

30

» Scripture

You have faithfully helped the followers of Christ, even when they were strangers to you.

■ 3 JOHN 1:5

» Pray

Loving Savior, though I am not always a faithful witness, I want to change for the better, to be more attentive to what you are asking of me, and to do these things in spite of difficulties that arise. Give me a courageous heart; give me a faithful heart.

» Act

Whatever difficulties I will face today, I will try to do so faithfully, letting Christ be my guide and inspiration.

Truth

"Truth and sin.
We must admit
that very often
lies are presented
to us with the
features of truth.
We must therefore
use our judge-
ment in recogniz-
ing truth, the
Word that comes
from God, and
repulse the temp-
tations that come
from the Father of
Lies."

✝ COMPOSTELA, 1989

» Scripture

I will ask the Father and he will give you another Advocate, to be with you forever. This is the Spirit of Truth.

■ JOHN 14:16–17

» Pray

Loving Savior, sometimes I feel bombarded by lies from the press, from commercials, from politicians. I believe that you are the source of all that is good and true. Open my heart that I might listen attentively to you. I need your gift of truth.

» Act

I will try to speak the truth in all that I say to others today, even when it is more convenient or expedient to lie.

"We are tempted to think that our spiritual journey and pastoral work depend on our actions and plans alone. But God, of course, invites us to cooperate with his grace, to invest all our resources of intelligence and energy in serving the cause of the Kingdom."

✝ ROME, 2001

» Scripture

Those who abide in me and I in them
bear much fruit, because apart from me
they can do nothing.

■ JOHN 15:5

» Pray

Loving Savior, the present culture
invites me to focus on myself and my
needs, and so it is difficult to acknowledge that I can do nothing without you.
Yet, I hope that I will never choose to
be apart from you. For this I need your
gift of grace.

» Act

I will take time today to write down
what I understand God's "grace" to be,
and I will try to discuss this with someone who shares my faith.

"We must learn not to be afraid, to rediscover a spirit of hope and a spirit of trust. Hope is not empty optimism…, but is rather the premise of responsible activity and is nurtured in that inner sanctuary of conscience where we are alone with God."

✝ NEW YORK, 1995

» Scripture

Keep alert, stand firm in your faith, be courageous, be strong.

■ 1 CORINTHIANS 16:13

» Pray

Loving Savior, I place my trust in you. Help me to stand firm in my faith and be nurtured in that "inner sanctuary" where I am never alone. Forgive me for the times I falter and help me to begin anew to trust in your loving promises.

» Act

I will try to be aware that God is with me in all I do today, and to pray often some simple words of trust.

"Love your families. Teach them the dignity of all life; teach them the ways of harmony and peace; teach them the value of faith and prayer and goodness! ...Help transform the world around you by giving the best of yourselves in the service of others and your country."

✝ JORDAN, 2000

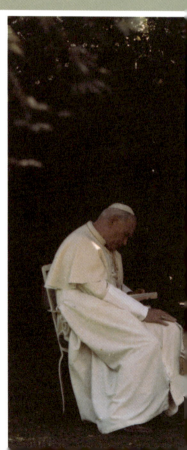

» Scripture

Do not be overcome by evil, but overcome evil with goodness.

■ ROMANS 12:21

» Pray

Loving Savior, from childhood I have been taught to "be good." I know now that goodness is much more than following rules; it comes from following you. Help me to bring harmony and peace to my family, my coworkers, my community, my country with your gift of goodness.

» Act

Today I want to offer Christ's gift of goodness to those around me, especially to someone I have difficulty with.

"How greatly today's world needs God's mercy! In every continent, from the depth of human suffering, a cry for mercy seems to rise up. …Mercy is needed to ensure that every injustice in the world will come to an end in the splendor of truth."

✝ BUENOS AIRES, 1987

» Scripture

Blessed are the merciful, for they will receive mercy.

■ MATTHEW 5:7

» Pray

Loving Savior, Son of the living God, have mercy on me, a sinner. In a special way I ask you today to have mercy on all in our world who are suffering. Hear their cries and protect them. Have mercy on me for forgetting their needs, which are far greater than my own.

» Act

I will make a deliberate effort to be merciful to others today, my children, coworkers, friends—in the same way God has mercy on me.

Humility

"Pride and the power of sin have made it difficult for many people to speak their 'mother tongue'. In order to sing God's praises we must re-learn the language of humility and trust, the language of moral integrity and of sincere commitment to all that is truly good in the sight of the Lord."

✝ ST. LOUIS, 1999

» Scripture

Beware of practicing your piety before others in order to be seen by them.

■ MATTHEW 6:1

» Pray

Loving Savior, everything you did was for God's Kingdom and for others. Help me to imitate you and learn again to speak my "mother tongue" of humility and trust that I too might live for God and others. Give me the gift of a humble heart.

» Act

Today I will try to do good things for others without expecting to be rewarded or applauded.

"Receive God's love gratefully… and be willing to give your lives every day for the transformation of history. Today, more than ever, the world needs your joy and service…, your strength and your commitment for the construction of a new society that will be more just and fraternal."

✝ BUENOS AIRES, 1987

» Scripture

With gratitude in your hearts, sing psalms, hymns, and spiritual songs to God.

■ COLOSSIANS 3:16

» Pray

Loving Savior, strengthen me to respond to the Holy Father's challenge to transform the world! I am overwhelmed by this prospect, but if you give me courage and a firm commitment, I will do all that I can. Please give me a grateful and determined heart.

» Act

When I say "thanks" to someone today, I will say it with the kind of gratitude that comes from the heart of Jesus.

45

"It is Jesus who stirs in you the desire to do something great with your lives, the will to follow an ideal, ...the courage to commit yourselves humbly and patiently to improving yourselves and society, making the world more human and more fraternal."

✝ ROME, 2000

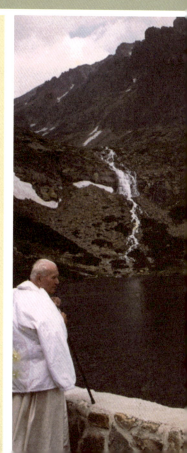

» Scripture

Grow in the grace and knowledge of our Lord and Savior Jesus Christ, to whom all glory belongs, both now and forever.

■ 2 PETER 3:18

» Pray

Loving Savior, true greatness comes from you and you alone can stir in me the desire to do something great with my life. Help me to respond to this call by serving others as you did and thus improving myself and my world.

» Act

Today I will think about the word "great" and who in my life I admire enough to call them great.

"Jesus teaches us to see the Father's hand in the beauty of the lilies of the field, the birds of the air, the starry night, fields ripe for the harvest, the faces of children and the needs of the poor and humble. If you look at the world with a pure heart, you too will see the face of God."

✝ DENVER, 1993

» Scripture

Blessed are the pure in heart, for they shall see God.

■ MATTHEW 5:8

» Pray

Loving Savior, I want with all my heart to see God's face. Help me to answer the Holy Father's challenge to be aware of all that is beautiful and good right before my eyes. Please open my mind and heart to recognize this great gift. Give me too a pure heart.

» Act

I will try to think like a child today, reacting to all the big and little miracles in my life as a child would. I will recall Jesus' words: Blessed are the pure in heart!

"Forgiveness is above all a personal choice, a decision of the heart to go against the natural instinct to pay back evil with evil.... It has its perfect exemplar in the forgiveness of Christ, who on the cross prayed: 'Father forgive them; for they know not what they are doing."

✝ ROME, 2002

» Scripture

Forgive us our trespasses as we forgive those who trespass against us.

■ MATTHEW 6:9–13

» Pray

Loving Savior, forgiveness seems like such a simple virtue, but when I examine my heart I find that I don't really forgive. I still carry the pain and resentment of the wrong others have done me. Give me please a truly forgiving heart.

» Act

Today I will focus on one person to whom I should offer forgiveness and I will resolve to let my act of forgiveness to be forever.

"My reasoned
conviction,
confirmed in
turn by biblical
revelation, is that
the shattered
order cannot be
fully restored
except by a
response that
combines justice
with forgiveness.
The pillars of
true peace are
justice and
forgiving love."

✝ ROME, 2002

» Scripture

The souls of the just are in the hands of God and no torment will touch them.

■ WISDOM 3:1

» Pray

Loving Savior, justice is such a remote-sounding virtue, and I tend to think of it as something dispensed by a judge. Help me to practice it in my daily life by dedicating myself to fairness, to mercy, and forgiveness. I need the gift of a just heart.

» Act

I will try today to practice justice by giving my time and attention more fully to those who depend on me at home and at work.

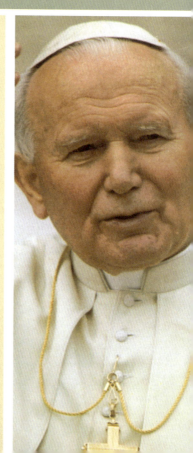

"Playing sports can encourage people to develop important values like loyalty, perseverance, friendship, and solidarity. In a way, sports are almost a 'sign of our times.' They have spread to every corner of the world, transcending differences between cultures and nations."

54 ✝ ROME, 2000

» Scripture

In a race all runners compete, but only one receives the prize. Run in such a way then that you might win an imperishable prize.

■ 1 CORINTHIANS 9:24

» Pray

Loving Savior, I am not such a good athlete, physically or spiritually, but I do want to win the imperishable prize of your grace. Strengthen me and guide me as I struggle to get spiritually fit. I need your gift of perseverance.

» Act

Today I will push myself when it comes to prayer and good works for others. I will renew my desire to win the prize.

"The contempla-
tion of nature
reveals not only
the creator, but
also our own role
in the world. In
order to have life
and have it abun-
dantly, in order to
re-establish the
original harmony
of creation, we
must respect the
divine image in all
of creation,
especially in
human life itself."

✝ DENVER, 1993

» Scripture

Consider the lilies of the field, how
they grow; they neither toil nor spin,
yet Solomon in all his glory was never
clothed as well.

■ MATTHEW 6:28–29

» Pray

Loving Savior, open my eyes that I might
truly contemplate all that you have creat-
ed. Help me to respect life in all its forms,
from the tiniest insect to the tallest tree;
from a baby in its mother's womb to the
elderly and infirm. May I both respect and
reflect your divine image in all my words
and actions.

» Act

I will try to be very conscious of the
miracles of people and nature that I see
today and I will offer praise.

"Listen to Jesus,
obey his com-
mandments,
commit yourself
to him. This is
the only formula
for a truly
successful and
happy life. Jesus
is also the one
source that gives
the deepest
meaning to life."

✝ ROME, 1998

» Scripture

Take my yoke upon you and learn from me, for my yoke is easy and my burden is light.

■ MATTHEW 11:29–30

» Pray

Loving Savior, in you I live and move and have my being. May I so commit myself to you and your Gospel that wherever I am, you are there too. When people see the good I do, may they praise and bless your holy name.

» Act

I will offer myself to Christ often today, at the same time asking for the strength to be a faithful and committed follower of his Gospel.

"If you really
wish to serve
your brothers and
sisters, let Christ
reign in your
hearts. Let him
strengthen you in
virtue and fill you
above all with his
charity. Let him
guide you along
the path that
leads to
holiness....
Do not be afraid
to be saints!"

✝ COMPOSTELA, 1989

» Scripture

Do you not know that you are God's temple and that God's Spirit dwells in you?

■ 1 CORINTHIANS 3:16

» Pray

Loving Savior, I want to be holy and I want you to reign in my heart, to be the center of my faith and of my life. Fill me with your charity and guide me that I might stay on the path to holiness. Give me the courage to be a saint.

» Act

I will try to do all things in the name of Christ today, remembering that he dwells in me and calls me to proclaim his Gospel in all that I do.

Index

14. Witness
Message for World Youth Day,
Rome 1996

15. Faithfulness
World Youth Day, Czestochowa,
August 1991 and World Youth Day,
Rome, August 2000

16. Truth
Speech to Youth on Monte
del Gozo, Compostela, Spain,
August 1989

17. Grace
Apostolic Letter Novo
Millennio Ineunte,
Rome 2001

18. Trust
Address to the 50th
General Assembly of the
United Nations Organization,
New York, October 5, 1995

19. Goodness
Homily, Amman Stadium,
Jordan, March 21, 2000

20. Mercy
World Youth Day,
Buenos Aires, Argentina,
April 11, 1987

21. Humility
Evening Prayer at St. Louis Cathedral,
Saint Louis, USA, January 27, 1999

22. Gratitude
Speech to Youth
World Youth Day, Buenos Aires
(Argentina), April 11, 1987

23. Greatness
Vigil of August 19 at Tor
Vergate, Rome 2000

24. Purity of Heart
Meditation for the Vigil,
5th World Youth Day,
Denver, USA, August 14, 1993

25. Forgiveness
Message for World Day of Peace,
Rome, January 1, 2002

26. Justice
Message for World Day of Peace
Rome, January 1, 2002

27. Perseverance
Homily, Jubilee of Sports,
Rome, October 29, 2000

28. Respect
5th World Youth Day,
Denver, USA, August 14, 1993

29. Commitment
15th World Youth Day
Rome 1998

30. Holiness
World Youth Day,
Compostela, August 1989